Deb & Randy
A Newbo

Such an exciting time for you both. Thank-you for letting us be a special part of it.

Love, Mom & Jim

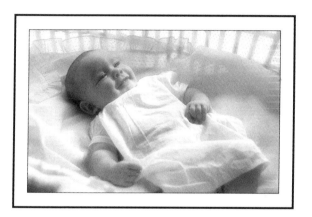

Joy A NEWBORN

Andrews and McMeel
A Universal Press Syndicate Company
Kansas City

ISBN: 0-8362-8052-0

Printed in Singapore

First U.S. edition

1   3   5   7   9   10   8   6   4   2

Edited by Linda Sunshine
Designed by Annemarie McMullan
Produced by Smallwood and Stewart, Inc.,
New York City

Credits and copyright notices appear on pages 94–95

Introduction

"Are not my children my favorite companions and most chosen friends?"

William Godwin, father of Mary Shelley

The birth of a baby is both a link to the past and a promise for the future. It's a reminder of the most powerful miracle life has to offer. "Family love is this dynastic awareness of time, this shared belonging to a chain of generations . . ." wrote Michael Ignatieff in *Lodged in the Heart and Memory.*

A Newborn Joy celebrates the wonder and miracle of welcoming a new life into the world. From the first ecstatic awareness of pregnancy though birth and the first days of life, the mysteries, delights and pleasures of the newborn infant are described in

poetry, letters and prose. Here are excerpts from the works of Maya Angelou, Laura Esquivel, Ann Tyler, Oscar Hijuelos, Amy Tan, Alice Hoffman, Joan Baez, Thomas Wolfe, Dorothy Parker, W. B. Yeats, William Blake, Percy Shelley and many others. Each quote is lavishly illustrated with fine art and photographs to make a memorable and cherished keepsake of this most profound passage of time.

"Life is the first gift," Marge Piercy once said, "love is the second, and understanding is the third."

Linda Sunshine

A world to be
born under your footsteps . . .

St. John Perse

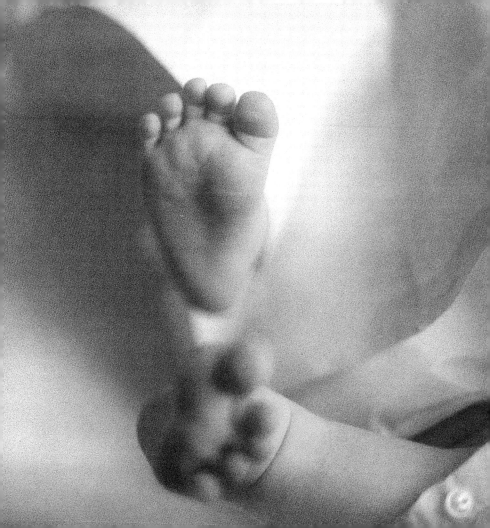

ut she sometimes felt a deep pleasure. A sense of elation would flow through her. She was not an intellectual or a saint, but she would look around and feel such a sweetness, such a connection with what she saw as the continuity of the world: all this would be passed on to the boy, everything that occurred within his endlessly diverting body, all that occurred out in the world. And it was that feeling that sustained her in the days when she was carrying the baby who would be their son.

Oscar Hijuelos
The Fourteen Sisters of Emilio Montez O'Brien

an I regard my pregnancy as anything but one long festival? We forget the anguish of the labor pains but do not forget the long and singular festival; I have certainly not forgotten any detail. I especially remember how at off hours sleep overwhelmed me and how I was seized again, as in my infancy, by the need to sleep on the ground, on the grass, on the sun-warmed hay. A unique and healthy craving.

Colette

Our birth is but a sleep and a forgetting:
The Soul that rises with us, our life's Star,
  Hath had elsewhere its setting,
    And cometh from afar:
  Not in entire forgetfulness,
  And not in utter nakedness,
But trailing clouds of glory do we come
    From God, who is our home:
Heaven lies about us in our infancy!

William Wordsworth
Ode: Intimations of Immortality

A Newborn Joy

I was breathing my Lamaze rhythms like a beached blowfish, and the doctor came in and told me to take it easy or I'd pass out long before delivery. I don't remember much after that. . . . They were wheeling me somewhere and the doctor kept saying, "Do you feel like pushing?" and I kept lying and saying no, because I was scared. I was hyperventilating, and I thought I heard a cat howling in the next room, but the nurses said it was me, and then finally I was pushing like mad. Oh God, I thought, I must be pushing a mountain out of me, and I heard the doctor say, "Looks like a healthy little boy," and I was wide awake and all ears and felt wonderful and had no pain and was crying and I wanted to see him. He was purple and gooey, but I reached up for him and started to sing, "Hello Little Friend," a Joe Cocker hit. They put him on my chest for a minute and I simply did not believe he was mine. . . . then [I] called David. "We got a Gabe," I told him. We had long since decided upon either Gabriel or Joaquin (we had no girl's name). . . . Born out of the sixties and out of our haphazard lives, born out of caring, born into our dreams, we had a Gabe.

Joan Baez
And a Voice to Sing With

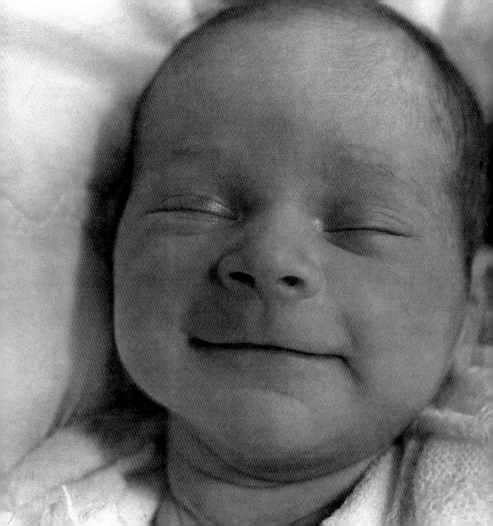

You were born to the joy of all:
the blue sky,
birds,
your mother's eyes.

Rabindranath Tagore

Tita was so sensitive to onions, any time they were being chopped, they say she would just cry and cry; when she was still in my great-grandmother's belly her sobs were so loud that even Nacha, the cook, who was half-deaf, could hear them easily. Once her wailing got so violent that it brought on an early labor. And before my great-grandmother could let out a word or even a whimper, Tita made her entrance into this world, prematurely, right there on the kitchen table amid the smells of simmering noodle soup, thyme, bay leaves, and cilantro, steamed milk, garlic and, of course, onion. Tita had no need for the usual slap on the bottom, because she was already crying as she emerged; maybe that was because she knew then that it would be her lot in life to be denied marriage. The way Nacha told it, Tita was literally washed into this world on a great tide of tears that spilled over the edge of the table and flooded across the kitchen floor.

That afternoon, when the uproar had subsided and the water had been dried up by the sun, Nacha swept up the residue the tears had left on the red stone floor. There was enough salt to fill a ten-pound sack ~ it was used for cooking and lasted a long time. Thanks to her unusual birth, Tita felt a deep love for the kitchen, where she spent most of her life from the day she was born.

Laura Esquivel
Like Water for Chocolate

$\mathscr{N}$ow join your hands,
and with your hands
your hearts.

William Shakespeare

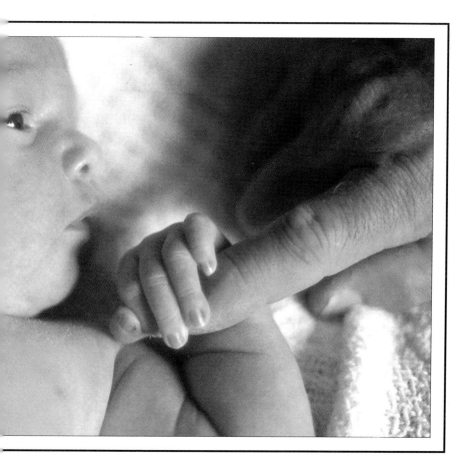

After a short labor, and without too much pain (I decided that the pain of delivery was overrated), my son was born. Just as gratefulness was confused in my mind with love, so possession became mixed up with motherhood. I had a baby. He was beautiful and mine. Totally mine. . . . Totally my possession, and I was afraid to touch him. Home from the hospital, I sat for hours by his bassinet and absorbed his mysterious perfection. His extremities were so dainty they appeared unfinished. Mother handled him easily with the casual confidence of a baby nurse, but I dreaded being forced to change his diapers. Wasn't I famous for awkwardness? Suppose I let him slip, or put my fingers on that throbbing pulse on the top of his head?

Mother came to my bed one night bringing my three-week-old baby. She pulled the cover back and told me to get up and hold him while she put rubber sheets on my bed. She explained that he was going to sleep with me.

I begged in vain. I was sure to roll over and crush his life or break those fragile bones. She wouldn't hear of it, and within minutes the pretty golden baby was lying on his back in the center of the bed, laughing at me.

I lay on the edge of the bed, stiff with fear, and vowed not to sleep all night long. But the eat-sleep routine I had begun in the hospital, and kept under Mother's dictatorial command, got the better of me. I dropped off.

My shoulder was shaken gently. Mother whispered, "Maya, wake up but don't move."

I knew immediately that the awakening had something to do with the baby. I tensed. "I'm awake."

She turned the light on and said, "Look at the baby." My fears were so powerful I couldn't move to look at the center of the bed. She said again, "Look at the baby." I didn't hear sadness in her voice, and that helped me to break the bonds of terror. The baby was no longer in the center of the bed. At first I thought he had moved. But after closer inspection I found that I was lying on my stomach with my arm bent at a right angle. Under the tent of blanket, which was poled by my elbow and forearm, the baby slept touching my side.

Mother whispered, "See, you don't have to think about doing the right thing. If you're for the right thing, then you do it without thinking."

She turned out the light and I patted my son's body lightly and went back to sleep.

Maya Angelou
I know why the caged bird sings

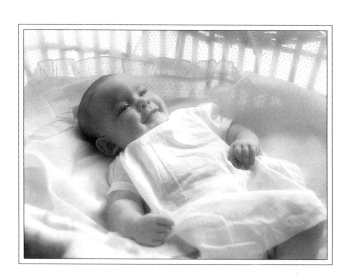

To the Newborn

Like a round loaf, that's how small you were.
I rolled you on the board with my palm,
I kneaded you, patted you,
greased you smooth, floured you,
I shaped your roly body.
You slept in the palm of my hands.
You'd hardly dawned, your slight bones
were still soft under your skin, yet
how vehemently your vulnerable life
pulsed in your tiny torso, your folded limbs
closed about you like thick petals,
beneath, you slept like the still of a rose.

Judit Toth

Some are born to

sweet delight . . .

William Blake

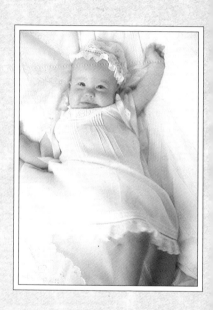

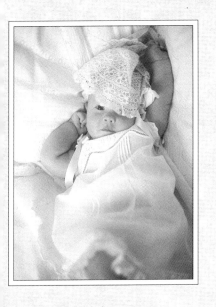

or nine long months she has carried this child in her body, and if she had not done so, he would not be there beside her now: a perfect and complete human being she can see and touch ~ his head, covered with soft, fine down; his pink sleepy face; his tiny clutched fists; his plump warmly wrapped body. She has had months of discomfort, weeks of illness and, finally, hours of agony; she would gladly go through every minute of all that again for the sake of this moment. . . . whatever happens in the future, nothing can rob her of the joy of that supreme hour; and when her baby is put in her arms and she holds him against her breast, she has another swift surge of joy if she knows he is still to draw on her for sustenance.

Frances Parkinson Keyes

ater that evening, as soon as his work was done, my father rushed out of the theatre, jumped into a cab, and was driven furiously homeward. The great stars glittered overhead, filling his heart with joy and ecstasy, his spirit was united to the timeless universe, he was annihilated and he saw nothing but glory everywhere, and he could hear the sounds of boats out on the river. When he got home he ran into the house and up the stairs. Bella held me in her arms, and when my father saw me, he cried:

"Her eyes are two black buttons and they are looking straight at me because she knows I am her father."

Outside the boats were blowing in the harbor, and great ships were putting out to sea.

Thomas Wolfe
The Good Child's River

Infant Joy

'I have no name;
I am but two days old.'
What shall I call thee?
'I happy am,
Joy is my name.'
Sweet joy befall thee!

William Blake

More than the gems
Locked away and treasured
In his comb-box
By the God of the Sea,
I prize you, my daughter.

Lady Ōtomo of Sakanone
Sent from the Capital to Her Elder Daughter

When Charlie first saw our child, our Mary, he said all the proper things for a new father. He looked upon the poor little red thing and blurted, "She's more beautiful than the Brooklyn Bridge." On subsequent viewing when we three were alone, he stared at her long and solemnly and then said an odd thing, "We have given her birth and death and that's about all we can give her, really." I thought it morbid at the time because I was feeling all-powerful, as women do after childbirth. He was right, of course. It was life that would give her everything of consequence, life would shape her, not we. All we were good for was to make the introductions. We could introduce her to sights and sounds and sensations. How these reacted on her we must leave to her own private self. It is hard to accept this background position, and like most parents, we did not do it very well at all times. But we did at least understand our roles, and that is a step toward a passing performance.

Helen Hayes
A Gift of Joy

Florence   April 30, [1849]

. . . There! ~ and almost done my paper without a single word to you of the *baby!* Ah, you wont believe that I forgot him, even if I pretend ~ so I wont. He is a lovely, fat, strong child, with double chins and rosy cheeks, and a great wide chest ~ undeniable lungs, I can assure you. Dr. Harding called him "a robust child", the other day, and "A more beautiful child he never saw"! ~ I never saw a child half as beautiful, for my part. We have had him vaccinated to everybody's satisfaction . . . Everything was as right as could be, and I heard Dr. Harding say to the nurse, "that in all his practice he had never seen the functions of nature more healthfully performed". . . .

your most affectionate
Ba

Elizabeth Barrett Browning

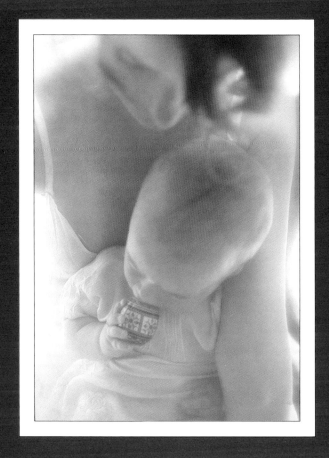

So for the mother's sake the child was dear,
And dearer was the mother for the child.

Samuel Taylor Coleridge

Adoption

I stitched us together by night
in the rocking chair, marveled
at your fingers, the foreign navel,
memorized the sweep of your eyebrows,
unraveled your language.
Having accepted the unfamiliar,
I kept watch
for proof of our union.

Tonight I inhale as I kiss
your perfect face, moist
from busy dreaming. Your fragrance
marks me ~ that fingerprint
only a parent can read.
I crawl in beside you, grateful
and patient, to dip us
with even breath
in this night's ink.

Alison Kolodinsky

hat was that fairy tale? "Sleeping Beauty," maybe, or "Snow White." Skin as white as snow and hair as black as coal and lips as red as roses. So she was prettier than most babies, yes, but still not all that interesting. Until she opened her eyes.

She opened her eyes and fixed Ian with a thoughtful, considering stare, and Ian felt a sudden loosening in his chest. It seemed she had reached out and pulled a string from somewhere deep inside him. It seemed she *knew* him. . . .

Anne Tyler
Saint Maybe

A Newborn Joy

A double blessing is a double grace.

William Shakespeare

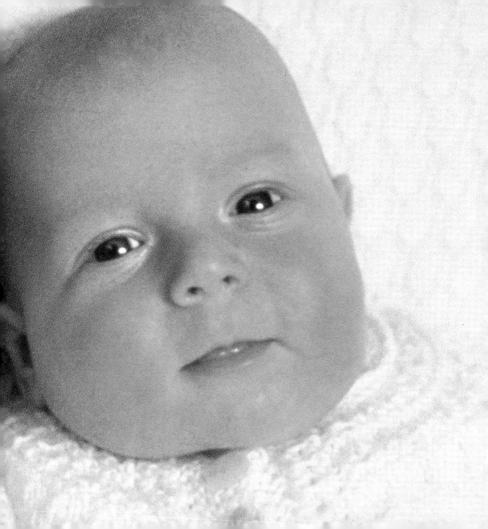

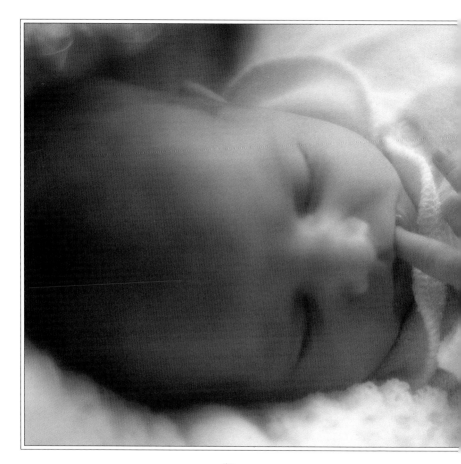

In her crib, the baby is falling asleep; she turns on her side and slips her thumb into her mouth and hums to herself the way she always does when she's tired. There are clean white pillowcases and sheets, washed so many times they're as soft as snow.

Alice Hoffman
Turtle Moon

Prayer for a New Mother

Let her have laughter with her little one;
   Teach her the endless, tuneless songs to sing,
Grant her the right to whisper to her son
   The foolish names one dare not call a king.

Dorothy Parker

Springfield Sep 17 1853

My dear Mrs Black

Mrs Remann sent me word to day, that your husband was here, & would leave in the morning for St Louis. May I trouble you to undertake the purchase of a white fur hat, for a boy of 6 months, I presume ere this, the fall styles have been received, I should like white trimmings & white feather, if you find any to your taste, of the prettiest quality. Would you be kind enough also, to have me a drawn satin bonnet made of this brown, lined with white, I have some small brown feathers for the outside, also inside trimming, which I suppose is not necessary to send down, please have it made to *your* taste, if fine black lace, will be used this fall, perhaps *that* would be pretty with it, for the outside. I can put the feathers & flowers inside my self. I send you a string for the size of the hat, ~ if I am not too troublesome, may I have them about the first of October? I should think a pretty hat, would cost about four dollars, but if more, I do not object, as it will *last all* my boys.

We would be much pleased to see you in Springfield, it appears a long time since you left. Will you excuse this hasty scrawl & believe me yours truly

Mary Lincoln

Bone of my bones,
and flesh of my flesh . . .

Genesis 2:23

And even though
I taught my daughter the opposite,
still she came out the same way!
Maybe it is because she was born to me
and she was born a girl. And I was
born to my mother and I was born a girl.
All of us are like stairs, one step
after another, going up and down, but
all going the same way.

Amy Tan
The Joy Luck Club

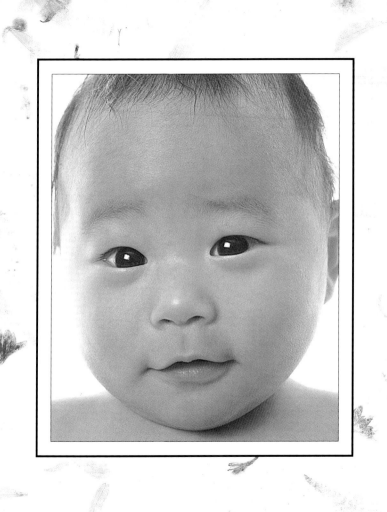

Mother's Song

If snow falls on the far field
where travelers
spend the night,
I ask you, cranes,
to warm my child in your wings.

Anonymous

I sigh that kiss you,
For I must own
That I shall miss you
When you have grown.

W. B. Yeats
The Angels Are Stooping

They say that thou wert lovely from thy birth,
Of glorious parents, thou aspiring Child.

Percy Shelley

place baby's first photograph here

*Y*OUR NAME

Your birth

Date and Time

Weight

Length

Hair and Eye Color

Hospital

Doctor

How you got your name

Names you nearly had

Tracing of Your Hand

Tracing of Your Foot

Newspaper Headlines on Your Birthday

*F*AMOUS PEOPLE BORN ON YOUR BIRTHDAY

$\mathcal{W}$HO VISITED YOU IN THE HOSPITAL

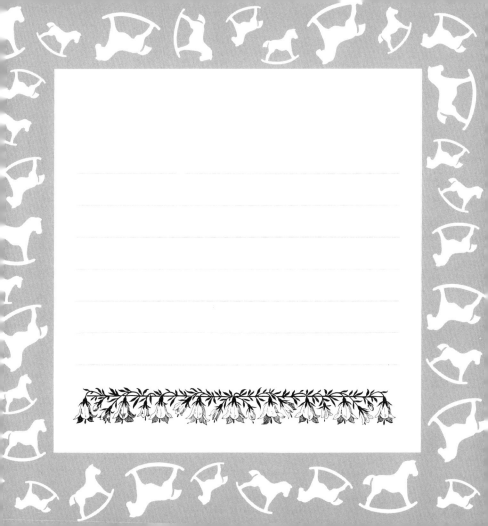

You and Your Mother

place photograph here

YOU AND YOUR FATHER

place photograph here

$\mathcal{Y}$OUR FIRST DAY HOME

Your first sounds

Your First Smile

GIFTS FOR YOU

Your Favorite Toys

$\mathcal{Y}$OUR FIRST OUTING

$\mathscr{A}$ DAY IN YOUR LIFE

wake up time

breakfast

play time

lunch

nap time

dinner

bath time

bedtime

Your First Holiday

_____

_____

_____

_____

_____

_____

_____

_____

Your Family

place photograph here

$\mathscr{Y}$OUR NEW MOVES

THE FIRST NIGHT YOU SLEPT THROUGH

$\mathcal{M}$Y HOW FAST YOU'VE GROWN

Age	Weight	Length

Acknowledgments

Excerpt from *The Fourteen Sisters of Emilio Montez O'Brien* by Oscar Hijuelos. Copyright © 1993 by Oscar Hijuelos. Reprinted by permission of Farrar, Straus & Giroux, Inc.

Excerpt from *Earthly Paradise* by Colette, edited by Robert Phelps. Copyright © 1966 by Farrar, Straus & Giroux, Inc. Reprinted by permission of Farrar, Straus & Giroux, Inc.

Joan Baez, *And A Voice to Sing With*. Copyright © 1987 by Joan Baez. Reprinted with permission of Summit Books, a division of Simon and Schuster, Inc.

From *Like Water for Chocolate* by Laura Esquivel. Copyright Translation © 1992 by Doubleday, a div. of Bantam Doubleday Dell Publishing Group, Inc. Used by permission of Doubleday, a division of Bantam Doubleday Dell Publishing Group, Inc.

Maya Angelou, *I know why the caged bird sings*. Copyright © 1969 by Maya Angelou. Reprinted with permission of Random House, Inc.

Judit Toth, "To the Newborn," translated by Laura Schiff. Reprinted in *Modern Hungarian Poetry*, edited by Miklos Vajda. Copyright Judit Toth. Reprinted with permission of Artisjus, Budapest, as agents for Judit Toth.

Frances Parkinson Keyes, *All Flags Flying, Reminiscences of Frances Parkinson Keyes*. Copyright © 1972 by Henry W. Keyes, Executor of the Will of Frances Parkinson Keyes. All Rights Reserved. McGraw-Hill, Inc. Reproduced with permission of McGraw-Hill, Inc.

Reprinted from *The Good Child's River* by Thomas Wolfe. Edited and with an Introduction by Suzanne Stutman. Copyright © 1991 by the University of North Carolina Press and the Estate of Thomas Wolfe. Used by permission.

Lady Ōtomo of Sakanouie, "Sent from the capitol to her elder daughter," from *The Penguin Book of Japanese Verse* translated by Geoffrey Bownas and Anthony Thwaite (Penguin Books, 1964) copyright © Geoffrey Bownas and Anthony Thwaite, 1964.

Helen Hayes, *A Gift of Joy*. Copyright © 1965, 1993 by Helen Hayes and Lewis Funke, reprinted by permission of the publisher, M. Evans and Co., Inc, 216 East 49th Street, New York, NY 10017.

Elizabeth Barrett Browning, *Women of Letters, Selected Letters of Elizabeth Barrett Browning and Mary Russell Mitford*. Copyright © 1987 by Meredith B. Raymond and Mary Rose Sullivan. Twayne Publishers, Boston. Original letter in the Wellesley College Library Special Collection, English Poetry Collection.

Art Credits